Forest School

Poems of Moss, Mind, and Mystery

Charles Ames Fischer

Forest School
Poems of Moss, Mind, and Mystery
by Charles Ames Fischer

Published by

SB
Sienna Books

ISBN: 978-1-940107-09-7 (Paper)

Book Design: Nick Zelinger, NZGraphics.com

First Edition

Published in the United States of America

In Memory of
My Mother, Judith Fischer

Introduction

When I was young, I thought of school as a place made of brick and bells, where learning happened in straight lines—row by row, book by book. But I have since come to understand that our deepest lessons often arrive unannounced, along the curved paths of curiosity. Like many in my generation, I spent a great deal of time outdoors and learned that nature is a teacher of the soul, a tuner of the spirit.

In the first section, *Moss,* the poems gather their wisdom from the woods. The earth is a classroom where we absorb the long-view lessons of stillness and softness. In the forest, we can find truth and serenity, though they are difficult to hold, as the wind revises everything.

The second section, *Mind,* is less about desks and chalk dust and more about what school should be. Formal education shapes us in helpful and harmful ways, but without a connection to nature, to awe and wonder, we are certainly incomplete. Every syllabus needs soul.

The third section, *Mystery,* looks onward and upward. These are poems of meditation, illumination, and instigation. Here, listening is made visible.

Lastly, it has not escaped my attention that the word *education* contains all five vowels. It suggests that learning is five-dimensional, more involved and interwoven than we often realize. Whether you read this book straight through or wander about, I invite you to step lightly. This is a school without walls. You are already enrolled.

Author's Note

This book is in memory of my mother, Judith Fischer, who supported me in every decision I made, good and bad. I wrote the second poem in this collection, *Uplift Walk,* for her when she passed several years ago. She has always loved walking, not only as a form of exercise but also to meet new people. Mom was never shy about striking up conversations with strangers. For her, that saying comes to mind: "A stranger is just a friend you haven't met." These words certainly encapsulate Mom's uplifting view of the world.

Mom would have liked this collection of poems, and I hope you do, too.

Judy Fischer

Forest School

Part I:
Moss

"In all things of nature there is something of the marvelous."

~Aristotle

Prelude to the Softer Side

What of winding trails and sacred tales,
    and forests dark and wide
Of ancient things and fairy rings,
    and adventures deep inside
Of soaring pines and spirit lines
    and a fire's intimate glow
Of bright birdsong and night dream-song,
    and the majesty of flow?

What of starry skies and wistful sighs,
    and woodlands thick and green
Of tuneful creeks and mountain peaks,
    and all the worlds between
Of serene ponds and mystic bonds,
    in all the realms unseen?

What of inner lives and woven lines,
    spirit-paths deep and long
Of nature's laws and stunning awe,
    and wonder, full and strong
Of finding calm and healing balms,
    and passion's guiding light
Of discover-play inside the Way
    with Purpose taking flight?

What of them? What of them?
    They are vitamins of Forest School
part of the Great Nurture and Need,
the tree rings of a strident life;
    they are development seeds.

We who embrace this special endeavor
    touch off sacred circles that expand
        forever
                forever
                        forever...

Uplift Walk

Go on an Uplift Walk
that would be my way.
Others may stomp around
or trounce heavy-footed down the trail.
I would choose
to go on an Uplift Walk.

It begins with altering your stride,
stepping light-footed with buoyancy
and a smile throughout the whole of you.
Then a deep sigh,
a gentle slowness and calm as you proceed,
opening your awareness to nature
and the unseen worlds
(humming or whistling optional).

Cherish this walk, for
there is Hope in the colors of a flower,
Uplift in the quiet sounds on the breeze,
Exhilaration in the shade of a tree,
Elation in the smoothness of a stone
to brighten and raise your spirits.
They are there, waiting to be seen
and appreciated.
Go on an Uplift Walk,
that would be my way.

Stars

innumerable lanterns
hang in the firmament

eons of light undertake
their long journeys to
grace these earthen eyes

radiant entreaties
stir the primordial
in celestial tides

call the yearning heart,
ring the inner bell.

In Quintessence

Elementally, life begins
With breaking water and first-air breath;
Ends with fire in eyes fading,
Marking earthly death.

Air is kite-flying on a summer day,
Water, the chill of a sprinkler's spray.
Earth is castles in sun-warmed sand,
Fire toasts s'mores by a camper's hand.

Fire is the warmth from a bed of coals,
Earth is the ground firm under soles.
Air is watching dandelion seeds float,
Water is buoyancy underneath a boat.

Water, a river that nourishes ground,
Air, the vibration that carries sound.
Fire is a candle for illumination,
Earth, the stone for strong foundations.

Earth is a meadow of colorful flowers,
Water, a thunder of heavy showers.
Fire is the flash in a coming storm,
Air gives a eulogy its final form.

Water may carry a body to sea,
Air scatters ashes, the soul flying free.

Fire purifies on a pyre's bright mound
Earth, the body held beneath ground.

Spiritually, the elements
Are but four universal keys.
From womb to tomb and then beyond,
nature is coded with mysteries.

Today's Magic

These woods have
many a bright fairy
-tale within them.

The daily goal is to
see with new eyes,
hear with fresh ears.

Adventuring past
a fastened gate,
you rescue a damsel
-fly from the pool.

It's vital to stay
true to your quest
-ions and honor
your imagination.

Later in the journey,
you admire a dragon
-fly hovering over
a planter of peonies.

On the trail to
the nearby pond,
you discover gold
-enrod and many
a precious jewel
-weed patch.

You gather each
separate element,
discover that they tell
a tale. Finally real
-ize you are the story.

A Song Too Long to Finish

To be a stream
is to move and keep on moving
motion apparent,
to feel water caress your mobility
to flow and perpetually go
feeling the coolness pass through
 to be a gift to all living things
to harmonize the contentment of the
eventual stillness that water seeks.

A stream is awake and alive,
water the gift, flow the deliverer.
Even dry riverbeds
remember, in dreams,
the shape of water.

To be a stream
is to be in the freedom
of perpetual giftings
passed along to all who seek the
wonders of water.
To be a stream,
slinging musical notes
from the mountain tops
all the way to the sea.

Fireflies

Tiny lanterns
stitching constellations
glowing poets
wandering nostalgia
winged deacons
flickering prayers.

To Be a Cloud

I   am   slowly   wisping   many   directions at once

neither   heavy   nor light

          shall   be carried   on the wind.   for I know my   weight

sometimes I   flow and   am flowed   I stir   and   am stirred   in multiplicity

          I churn   and am   churned   gliding on bands of air:

                              watching others   sail

drift apart   sometimes   disperse into emptiness.

                                        Other times I

compress   and am   compressed   into thickened density.

                                        I feel the heaviness then

as I gather stormy grey

          until gravity   pulls   and   pulls

                                        and I relent

24

release   and am   released

                falling to the   ground far below

                            in tiny beads.

I feel   relief   and am   relieved

                      the weight finally gone.

    On some   of these occasions   I hold together   am held

by the softness of the air   so gentle   and   soothing.

        I do   not like these

                thunderous moments

so terribly sudden in their

finality.   It's far too easy

                to disappear forever, and

                    some day I will drift

    and be   drifted for the last

                time.

We Can Be Marvelous Together

*"In every walk with nature one receives
far more than he seeks."*
                    ~John Muir

Hi, sparrow, could you spare some inspiration?
   Which constellations rule your feathers?
Oh, crow, where is your cache of cleverness?
   What maps are hidden in your eyes?

Hello, oak, could I have some of your might?
   How do you hold onto firmament?
Howdy, ivy, how about a twist of tenacity?
   How do you ascend on moon threads?

Don't worry, I pay back for my existence—with interest.
   Curiosity is my trade, wonder my coin,
and I'll swap you for surveillance.
   I see you and I hear you and I marvel.

The sparrow flits closer. The crow caws.
   The oak creaks and the ivy trembles
We exchange a tangle of amazement—
   what moves through me moves through all.
Now you are more you and I am more me;
   this is how one and one make three.

A Step in the Right Direction

Greetings Another, I am NORTH
and I wear the black cloak of night.
I am where roots grow unseen,
where compelling ideas gestate.
I am the patience of winter,
the moon-silence of midnight.
My soft lights offer contemplation.
Sacred am I, for I am eternity.

Greetings Another, I am EAST
and my words are verdant.
I am the enlightening dawn,
the airy excitement of arisings.
I am the well being of spring,
the honesty of sunrise promises.
Look to me for joy and hope,
for I am the wand of the future.

Greetings Another, I am SOUTH
and my words are lush and alive.
I am the fire of midday summer,
the red courage of refinement.
I am the power of passion,
the potency of high principles.
Look upon me for strength,
for I am the sword of the present.

Greetings Another, I am WEST
and I am silver-white twilight.
I am the vision quest veil,
the deep waters of mystery.
I am the vespers of harvest,
the twilight freedom of peace.
Look to me for compassion,
for I am the nightfall past.

The Process of All Things

An acorn does not become another acorn.
   It may decompose, it may get eaten,
but its destiny is to become an oak.

An oak does not become another oak.
   It may collapse, may become diseased,
but its destiny is to create acorns.

Acorns do not become other acorns.
   They may fall, they may crumble open,
but their destiny is to become a forest.

The Oak Speaks

I am an oak

I am an oak
  long have I stood here

I am an oak
  long have I stood here
  on the land of my ancestors

I am an oak
  long have I stood here
  on the land of my ancestors
  in the soil churned by kindred roots

I am an oak
  long have I stood here
  on the land of my ancestors
  in the soil churned by kindred roots
  feeling the cool earth shiver

I am an oak
  long have I stood here
  on the land of my ancestors
  in the soil churned by kindred roots
  feeling the cool earth shiver
  lifting branches, curling my leaves

I am an oak
  long have I stood here
  on the land of my ancestors
  in the soil churned by kindred roots
  feeling the cool earth shiver
  lifting branches, curling my leaves
  raising praises to the sun

I am an oak
  long have I stood here
  on the land of my ancestors
  in the soil churned by kindred roots
  feeling the cool earth shiver
  lifting branches, curling my leaves
  raising praises to the sun
  releasing gratitude

I am an oak
  long have I stood here
  on the land of my ancestors
  in the soil churned by kindred roots
  feeling the cool earth shiver
  lifting branches, curling my leaves
  raising praises to the
  sun releasing gratitude
  shading the younglings

I am an oak
   long have I stood here
   on the land of my ancestors
   in the soil churned by kindred roots
   feeling the cool earth shiver
   lifting branches, curling my leaves
   raising praises to the sun
   releasing gratitude
   shading the younglings
   grandmothering the forest.

Winter Speaks

I am Winter, Ruler of The Long Night,
Keeper of the Twilight Keys,
Ward of the Eternal Renewal
And I wish to say to you:

It is my cold that encourages your warmth,
So hang up your gloves and scarves,
Arrange your weary feet near the fire
In the log cabin calm of my long nights.

My frosty winds whorl the air with snow—
One of water's only chances to repose,
To dream crystalline dreams before
The eventual journey to the sea.

My emptiness provides fulfillment,
Allows all to curl and consolidate,
To merge and manifest
In my gentle stillness and silence.

It is my serenity that gives rise
To evergreen opportunities
That will rouse from dormancy
And spring to life in the months ahead.

In the winter of your whole lifespan
Aged and gray, a shadow of yourself outside,
You are crystal-strong and resolute,
Fortified with stories and wisdom within.

Know that these are but some of my gifts to you
And know that you will season well.

An Ode to Squirrels

To the squirrels of the world
   thank you for your joyful play
      with your tails all puffy and curled;
      you always make my day.

Spiraling around the tree
   playing a game of hide-and-seek
      keeping yourselves safe from me
      Ah, you're such crafty sneaks!

Oh, you marvelous shadow-tails!
   With your cute acorn-fat cheeks
      scurrying along tree branch trails
      I could watch you play for weeks.

Pouncing and jumping through leaves
   searching for your caches of food.
      You always forget where to go
      But that's how the forest grows!

To the squirrels of the world
   thank you for your silvery way
      with your tails all fluffy and swirled,
      you always make my day.

Autumn, at the Edge of Consequence

Even nouns are a process

that raindrop was once part of a stream
      the tear on your cheek was
a drop in the ocean, an ocean in a drop

that pencil in your hand was part of a tree
      its point scratching out cursive
made of graphite and clay

eventually, every rock will roll through
          igneous
metamorphic   sedimentary
on its way to stardust

prisoners are always caged by two cells
      the body, the mind
the walls we build, the walls we carry
      inside and outside

Truth is always upstream
      as salmon know well
all things return to the source
      of their arising

still, even evolution evolutes
      it's not that things disappear
but they return differently

poems never actually end, they just

Forest Ghazal

In the beginning, all I found was a growing forest,
a simple grouping of trees, just an ongoing forest.

But I continued exploring there, learning as I grew;
what was wilderness became an easygoing forest.

Then the wisdom of altering my stride, sacred-stepping,
until the very same place became a slowing forest.

I began to notice the many subtle lives woven
into the breathing tapestry of the flowing forest.

In the slow inner stillness there is peace and harmony;
with new eyes to see, I discovered a glowing forest.

Oh, so majestic, my heart and soul full of gratitude,
I thank you for all the gifts you are bestowing, Forest.

Part II:
Mind

"Look deep into nature, and then you
will understand everything better."

~Albert Einstein

School

When our circles became squared,
we found ourselves indoors, flatly
staring, wondering where the beauty
and the flow went. Inside, we lost the
enzymes of play and discovery.

We found ourselves in buildings,
sitting in unnatural rows like farmed
trees or compacted into painful carrels
and wrecked tangles of personal space,
all awkward elbows and knees.
We could only shrink in accommodation.

Hard edges cut, we were boxed,
protracted with inside instruction,
staring out windows with curiosity:
When can we go outside? The bell!
Suddenly we rushed the doors, split
into the freedom of the playground.

The angles were lost on us, except a
vague forward rationale of blah, blah,
high school…something, something…
adulthood. Mostly, we conformed.
Ghostly, we responded. But we never
got to ask our graver questions,
which would have called for spirals.

Summer Camp in the '80s

At camp, in the woodlands of upstate New York,
we collected acorn caps, pinecones, and bits of moss,
found garter snakes, millipedes, and water striders.
We squealed with delight and disgust digging through
rotten stumps and logs, discovering earwigs and ants,
roly-polies and silverfish. I remember chasing
dragonflies and grasshoppers, fireflies and ladybugs.

I recall the improbability of a saddleback caterpillar,
the strangeness of a praying mantis or spotted salamander,
the weirdness of weevils. Those were the wonderful
days of beetles and bees and butterflies.

I enjoyed the cooing of the mourning doves,
the haunting hoots of a great horned owl,
the chorus of crickets. I remember the smell
of mint and juniper, the earthy aroma released
when summer rain pelted dry dirt.

I remember worrying about snapping turtles and the
possibility of a rattlesnake. I was scared of skunks,
marveled at muskrats and beavers, enjoyed the hijinks of
raccoons and squirrels. I believed the myth that
the Daddy Longlegs was the most venomous spider
in the world, but its fangs were too small to bite people.
I believed in snipes and still wonder about fairies.

But now, who can even find fossils anymore?
Who sees sprites? Who catches a firefly in cupped hands
and whispers a wish before setting it free? Who even
climbs trees or nibbles on wintergreen berries?
Standing on Mother Earth, does anyone pluck petals from
a flower and wonder if *She loves me, she loves me not?*

Prayer to Childhood

Greatness, make me an instrument of curiosity.

Where there is the mundane, let me discover the unusual.
Where there is weariness, renew my gaze to ponder.
Where doubts cloud insight, rekindle my passion.
Where focus is lost, let me rediscover my childhood wonder.
When distractions arise, may I recall my resolve.

O Greatness, grant that I may unearth the extraordinary,
And through inquiry find the lore deep within:
To learn of the creation mysteries,
To attend to the outliers and oddities,
To weave together the ordinary and the astonishing

Into moment-by-moment experiences
So that my new normal
Is awareness and awe unbounded, unbound.

Concentric Circles

Listening is a creational gift,
forging connections between
people, ideas and the unknown.
To listen is to be silent,
to fashion active vacancy for
dialogue, exchange, expansion.

Meanings exist in people, not things;
a good listener is a midwife.

Writers feel the impulse for art
and create readers in the process.
But it's listeners who create speakers;
without an audience,
people are just thinkers.

To listen is to create inlets where
agreements can gather in safety.

What do we listen with? Ears, certainly.
Yet the skin is the largest organ in the body.
Sound enters the ear,
vibrates the tympanic membrane,
is amplified inside until hair cells
eventually create electrical impulses to
send to the awaiting brain.
Is it all that different than the

hairs on our skin?
We can, in fact,
listen with our whole bodies.

We all have filters, triggers, and biases,
but pure listening transcends
those walls of interference.

The goal of listening is not to confirm
what we want to hear, but to discover
new understandings in ourselves and others.

What do we listen with? Sentiments hopefully.
We can always choose to listen for what is
wrong and bad or for what's right and good
on a moment-by-moment basis.

We listen to *do better,* but more
importantly, we listen to *be better.*
And beyond those implications:
Could it be we are the ears of God?

The Point

the old ways are mostly gone now but they echo in the earth
i hear fragments of them as i pass through this land

along Lower Sylvan Pass i suddenly sense an arrowhead
and gently dig it free from the cool soil

the point is chipped but the edges are still sharp and strong
i stroke the ridges and valleys with my fingers

i hold the stone to my cheek, feel the maker in the marks
his hands too were thick and steady

i can tell the stone came from Obsidian Cliff where Blue Creek
descends into what is now called Norris

this arrowhead has history: it sliced into the heart of a deer
by Dunanda Falls, grazed a bison near Rainbow Point

and in a small glade on Pitchstone Plateau felled an elk—
what some First Peoples called *hexaka* or *unpan*

some would imprison this point in the walls of a museum
many would look for more to sell

but there is not enough of the sacred in this world
i return it to Earth and let its echo endure

My Listening Stone

The summer I turned ten
   I had to stay with   my Grandpa in the country.

   He lived in a cottage   at the end of a dusty road,
      long after the highway ended
                           and streets lost their names.
It was a lovely place,
   full of wildflowers, dragonflies   and unsung songs.
      At first I didn't like the silence,
         being far from the humming city
                     and my neighborhood friends.

I grew to love the quiet,   the sighing slowness, and my
   wandering wonders   while I learned the land
      and the land learned of me.

      That summer of climbing trees   and skinned knees,
I made many friends, as only   children are able to do.

I danced with hummingbirds,   chased squirrels,
   listened to the evening chorus of frogs,
                        and sang with robins.

            I slept under white pines
and climbed tall maples, broad oaks.   I discovered the
   tang of blackberries,   the sweet smell of dandelions,
         and the marvel of mint tea.

That summer of remote wonders
Grandpa pulled me aside,   a smile on his face.

"You are ready to find a listening stone,"
he said with a glimmer in his eye. "Aye, today's the day."

"You'll know it when you find it.
It will call to you as obvious as if it leapt into your pocket.
Now, off you go!"

With a spring in my step and
awe in my eyes and ears,   I bounded away without a word.

I searched for the stone, crawled
under bushes and   snaked through grass,
          upended rocks and squished through mud.

I picked up dozens of rocks   some heavy,
      some tiny and light   in my small tomboy hands.
   Others sparkled in the sun,
              held strange patterns   and shapes.

But none of them called to me
and I went home empty-handed,   scruffy as a rowdy dog.

Grandpa nodded when I returned   and we ate dinner
   in silence,
          though later that evening he told
                    stories around the fire like usual.

The next morning I was up   at dawn,
skipping and jumping   across the countryside.

That summer of dancing fireflies,
          I knew I wasn't supposed to go past
                    the mossy stone wall by the creek.
But I felt the call of my stone nearby,
          knew it as surely as water flows.

          I hopped the wall, followed the song of my stone,
so insistent and clear.   It was small, smooth on all sides
     and gray so pale it was almost blue.

          A perfect puzzle piece in my palm,
it was strangely warm, as though
                    a tiny candle burned within.

          I hurried back to Grandpa's cottage
where he was waiting outside, warmth glowing on his face.

          I reached out to show him my treasure,
but he shook his head quickly
                    and clasped his hands around mine.

          "A listening stone is for you alone. Tell it your
hopes and dreams, your secret fears and innermost ideas.
          It will listen always with ease and openness.
It will hold your deepest secrets
                    and never, ever betray you."

So I bounded away without a word
and I've still never shown   anyone my special stone.

That summer of juicy berries, I slowly told it everything my
anxious mind could imagine.

And in a strange way, you could say
we became friends, my listening stone and I,
though I have another name for it now
and understand it never was about the stone.

Vowels

Beneath a cursive moon,
vowels emerge from shadows low.
With a swash of tails,
the pack hunts, lines flow.

Through empty pages they roam.
In essence, they are wild and free,
mysteries wrapped in spur and spine,
taper and terminal.

Alpha leading by link and loop,
the others kerning, finial and flag,
stress, strain and stroke
in the quietude of pale hours.

A, the apex, arc of ancient wisdom.
E, the eye, energizes and encompasses.
I, the imperium, for self and sun.
O, the bowl, for soul and earth.
U, the magnet, for weight and moon.

Social and territorial,
they hunt by bracketing prey,
ringing the weak, seeking legs and joints,
ligatures and necks.

They are often nocturnal and,
contrary to popular belief, do not howl
at the moon. Their vocalizations vary widely:
breathy, aspirated, even voiceless.

Beneath a cursive moon,
vowels emerge from shadows low.
With a swash of tails,
the pack hunts, lines flow.

A Walk About

"One touch of nature
makes the whole world kin."
    ~William Shakespeare

Life is more than concrete and glass,
        smoke and toxicity,
the gridlock of commuting or thinking.

Going for a walk is a boundless freedom,
a surrender to reception.
Partake now of a wisdom and a discipline:
b r e a t h e d e e p,
    d e e p e r   s t i l l
Soak in the blue meander of sky
the yellow verve of sun
the green majesty of grass.
No mere gaze, don't let your vision
slide off the edges—
                        ingest them to capacity,
fill your being with their vibrancies.

Envision their vital iotas coursing through
your blood, delivered to every cell
along with scarlet-enabled oxygen.
The body wants red, but parts of you
thirst for blue, yellow, green.

Calm the vortices of the mind,
                    expand,
witness what is around you:
                    See that tree?
             Experience it,
feel the tree-ness permeating,
your supplicant stillness
circulating through, around you.
No mere gaze, don't let your vision
slide off the edges—
                    observe,

             speak
each name as a spell upon
your anxieties and depressions,
focus on the abolition of hesitation
      with constancy and concord:

"Tree......dandelion......staircase......sidewalk...
chair......grass......bench......table......chair......chair...
sign......restaurant......leaf......house......leaf......person...
tree......bottle......tree......acorn......person......dog...
house......grass......fence......cloud......tree..."

Steady steady on. Steady on.
    Steady steady on. Steady on.
          Steady steady on. Steady on.

Resolve to find the grace of harmony,
the peaceful adhesion of kind,
aggregate your will toward perseverance,
self-locked internal and external placidity.

We do not have to participate in
the human race, the race,
that race toward frenzy and turbulence.
No, not the human race,
for we are human beings,
designed for being
　　　　alert...aware...aligned...active. Alive.

What Trees Have Taught Me

"I took a walk in the woods and
came out taller than the trees."
    ~Henry David Thoreau

I have learned to stay rooted in what is important;
    reaching up requires staying grounded,
and bending and breaking are very different outcomes.
    There is a need for stillness, and
to hold things forever requires the patience of amber.

I have learned the importance of capturing sunlight
    for the poetry of change and growth;
to stay evergreen even through the harshest winters
    and deciduous only on occasion,
dying to those aspects of myself no longer needed.

I have learned to be singular, but with others of kind who
help to forge the forest.
Some take the brunt of the wind and rain, others break
fires, repel insects.
Collectively, we must stay interconnected.

We acorns of actualization, pinecones of possibility
    all require the richness of soil
to discover what is beyond our seedling selves.
    We grow with the nutriment of
nature nurturing us through many seasons.

To Be Suddenly

People describe themselves many ways:
tall, smart, married.
Me, I am suddenly.

Suddenly is a moment-by-moment
love affair, living as a movie
rather than a photograph.

An impression incomplete, I am
suddenly a painter adding
to an unfolding canvas.

A song lingering unsung, I
am a busker suddenly at the
corners of Now and Soon.

A forest unhealthy, suddenly
am I a caretaker of the old,
guardian of the new.

Here, I am a poet spelunking
the creative darkness of
the suddenly arriving.

I am fifty sudden years old,
but sometimes I am not yet born,
and only rarely am I dead.

Suddenly I am inspired,
then the moment gone, I return
to chasing the sun.

Being suddenly takes discipline;
the goal: being open and ready,
willing and able to respond.

I am suddenly a scarecrow
in the fields of tomorrow, waving
away the crows of yesterday.

I am suddenly a kite let go
rising higher than expected,
trusting the wind.

I am the note that lingers
at the end of a light song
and then, suddenly silence.

Natural Impressions

Moab, Utah

Here nature is such an artist:
water carves rock into timeless canyons,
wind shapes sand into dunes,
arches frame the cloudy sky.

The earth is recurrently embossed,
green with scrub oaks and wild grasses,
painted with sunflowers and daisies
on a canvas of red rocks and soil.

In the Welcome Center museum
there's a glass sculpture—
a lightning bolt fusion of sand into glass,
a flash of power made fragile.

My thoughts spark and scatter—
enlightening bolts etch the mind.
Fleeting ideas form and fracture,
emboldened but delicate.

Kind words and deeds are uplifting,
imprint the mind with care.
But memories erode, leaving us
with arroyos waiting to refill.

The inner landscape shifts as surely
as the world blending around us.
At the end of your impressive life,
only what's engraved remains.

anyone went to a silver why school

anyone went to a silver why school
(with yes so questing many bright jewels)
earth   air   water   fire
he ignored his couldn't followed his could

.

Teachers and tutors (both squat and tall)
cared for anyone all by all
they shared their passions they pooled their same
wind   sand   birds   rain

other children followed (more than a few
and excited they got as up they grew
fire   earth   air   water)
so everyone learned more by more

serene in now they climbed the trees
they laughed in joy they raced the breeze
all by know and stirring still
anyone's any was new to them

someones learned to be everyones
sang their maybes and danced their woulds
(search play find and then) they
learned their evers and lived their dreams

sand   birds   rain   wind
(and only the few can begin to explain
how children are apt to learn to remember
with yes so questing many bright jewels)

one day anyone graduated
(and big one proudly pinned his ribbon)
caring folk cheered for all each by each
little by little and mind by mind

all by all and gleam by gleam
and more by more they lived their dreams
anyone and everyone sky beyond june
free as spirit and all by yes.

Teachers and tutors (both just and fair)
water   fire   earth   air
pooled their passions and went by same
wind sand birds rain

The Alchemy of Numbers

Life is a forest circling the sun—
when the circle's complete—zero turns one.
Just as A is followed by B, C, D
Creation emerges: one becomes three.

Study the natural laws, interpret the signs
the universe is constructed by special design.
Discover how things work, learn to count anew
not one-two-three, but one-three-two.

The first triangle will establish stability,
a foundation built on a trinity.

Four will begin a seasonal rotation,
forces working in coordination.
Five arises through *Spin and Pitch*
exponential growth, everything enriched.

Six is summoned, a resonant call
eternal harmony above all.
Two sacred triangles working in tow,
another law in operation: *As Above, So Below.*

The second triangle reheats, brings warmth from above,
high force descends; this is the meaning of love.

Seven is the leaven, begins the baking.
Eight is the gate, there for the taking.
Nine is the shrine, full of gold.
Have Gold to Get Gold: the law is old.

The third triangle is hallowed and must be earned.
Study *The Natural Laws;* they're waiting to be learned.

Poem of Gratitude for Some of My Favorite Teachers

Thank you, Earth, for teaching me the joy of climbing trees,
    how to admire a lone dandelion.
Air, for teaching me to sing, blow bubbles,
    and how to whistle even in the rain.
Fire, for teaching me respect, the benefits of caution
    and the power of passion.
Water, for teaching me to find the balances in all things
    and that there are many types of tears.

Thank you, Blue, for teaching me that calm and quiet
    are often only a sigh away.
Red, for teaching me how to stay focused within the
    chaos of these shifting times.
Turquoise, for the reminders that curiosity and wonder
    are just around the corner of my mind.
Yellow, for teaching me what a gift a smile can be.

Thank you to Crayons and Paper for teaching
    me the beauty of scribbling
        and for igniting my imagination;
to Graph Paper and Mechanical Pencil for helping
    me construct more creativity,
and to Origami for demonstrating that
    absolutely everything has potential.

And a most special acknowledgment to Up
    for helping me to see not only
        the sun, moon, and stars,
but also human development and possibility.

Star Wise

When people observe stars as radiant,
　　other bodies become dim.
When people see planets as hot, other
　　objects become cold.

Light and darkness define each other.
　　Near and far create each other.
Beginning and ending follow each other.
　　Space and time depend on each other.

Therefore, the Guide
　　observes without expecting,
teaches without concluding.

Stars shine, and she allows their brilliance;
　　stars fade, and she releases them.
She admires without possessing,
　　encourages without controlling.

When her guidance is done,
　　she casts it into the darkness
and unremembers everything;
　　that is why it lasts forever.

The Collective Endeavor

Each year in the early spring, the villagers
gathered by the huge oak in the field behind
McGroarty's barn for the annual walkabout.
After many hearty hellos, everyone separated
in the morning light to do their share.
The grown-ups organized the festivities,
the games and food, the tables and chairs.

As children, we had to gather wood for
the bonfire, an immense mountain
to burn hot and bright. First, we collected
twigs and sticks and branches—every nearby
loose bit of wood. But it was never enough.
Soon we ranged out farther and farther until
each armful was an adventure.
Eventually, in desperation, we'd hang from
dead branches until they snapped and
drag our heavy prize to the pile.
Or we'd wrestle small stumps loose and
roll them awkwardly over. By early afternoon
we often had enough and we'd finally get
to rest in the shade with fresh glasses of
iced tea or lemonade.

The elders had the most difficult work,
taking many hours to gather each NO around
the village until their bags were full
and they would hobble back to the barn.

NOs were difficult to carry, but the elders,
patient and steadfast, always managed.
They would carefully set their bags in a pile
near the bonfire and then settle in
to rest and tell stories.

In the late afternoon came the feast.
It was the one day a year we could truly say we were
spoiled. The older children and teens knew the secret:
don't eat too many sausages

or biscuits, hamburgers or hotdogs, don't fill
your plate with heaps of potato salad
or mounds of coleslaw. No, the secret was
to be patient—even if we were drooling
like newborns. Eventually came the desserts:
towering cakes, pyramids of warm muffins,
tubs of ice cream, trays of cookies fresh
from neighboring ovens. And best of all,
McGroarty's special family recipe
for Double Apple Pie.

Around dusk, when all the feasting was over,
when the seams of our clothes were fixing to bust,
everyone would circle around the bonfire.
One of the elders would say a few things
before lighting it up with a special match.
The bags of NOs would get passed around
and the children, teenagers included, would
take turns tossing a NO in the fire,

watch it sparkle and pop like tiny fireworks.
We'd watch the glowing embers rise into
the night sky and disappear amongst the stars.
Sometimes a NEVER was in one of the bags
and it would sizzle and spark and raise
quite a ruckus. But honestly, those
were always joyful surprises.

Near the end of the ceremony,
when the last NO was tossed in,
one of the elders would always ask:
"What do you want to be when you grow up?"
And we would all answer: "YES!"

Part III:
Mystery

"The clearest way into the Universe is through a forest wilderness."

~John Muir

Reveilations

Distance and mist make beauty;
half a mountain more attractive than a whole.
No artist would want it otherwise,
for the soul is too subtle
and fusion too powerful
to lift every veil.

True mysteries are veiled and re-veiled,
content to be illumined in layers.
The sacred is enshrined,
beautifully distant
and full of diversities.

An idea or a cadaver may be dissected,
but it is not possible to understand
the mystical living.
The opening of a sanctuary
will always find it empty.

Even words and actions wear veils;
half an idea more attractive than a whole.
No poet would want it otherwise,
for the universe is too subtle
and ions too positive
to lift every veil.

The Old Listeners

Was it a story whispered once,
   or a knowing just arrived—
that one of your great-grandparents
   was a Sereene, a Listener,
who traveled village to village
   l istening the corn to grow faster,
communing with injured animals,
    finding the song of water in parched soil.

The elders could listen the
   wind into the palms of their hands
and interpret the messages therein.
   They could listen melodies into being,
encourage poems to shed shyness,
   stones to spill their tribal secrets.

It is said that the Sereenes could
   even listen starlight into bending
a restorative path to Earth.
   Perhaps this is why, looking up
into the night sky, you can clearly hear
   the empty spaces sighing.

Collecting Silence

In a field where daisies sway,
I watch each petal unfurl into a poem.
Time slows,
somewhere a galaxy spins.
Silence here is soft,
the kind that settles on the skin.

At the ocean's edge,
silences are quick and heavy,
weighted pulses between waves.
Unless you're a collector,
they're easy to miss
in the constant motion.

On a mountaintop,
silence is sharp and frosty,
impossible to hold,
even in the isolated stillness.
It comes and goes on the wind
like the ghost of an eagle.

The forest offers another kind:
cool, layered silence, alive
with tiny, fragile movements.
It is a silence that listens back,
connective and inspiring,
full of gratitude.

Midnight snow falls in a silence
all its own, gentle and peaceful.
I don't even want to breathe
on such nights, but I know
that is the strain of silence
that awaits me in the grave.

Fire-by-Friction

With a spindle and a fireboard,
a bow and a handhold,
I begin a sacred act.

Apply pace and pressure,
slowly at first, building speed.

The goal is to produce a gravity of dust,
a nebula of potential.

With enough force and friction,
an ember emerges:
a tiny star.

A little nursing, some feeding,
this light squeezed
out of the wood

radiates warmly to life;
its solar self ignites
here on our planet.

Transcendence

*"I believe a leaf of grass is no less
than the journey-work of the stars."*
~Walt Whitman

Absorbed in the grandfather
clock of life, things do not change
much in our cognizance.
Life evolves quickly relative
to a geologic timepiece,
mostly imperceptible to us.
We intervolve together,
collectively as a species,
the critical mass sluggishly
sliding into transcendence.
Each generation plays with
a ration of genes, hoping to get
the formula right for the next
expansive upgrade.

The baby learns the inch
before the foot or yard;
the child learns the minute
before the looming hour;
the youth experiences
sand and concrete
before mental abstracts.

The teen focuses on the one
before appreciating the many,
and the adult gains all
without losing a second.

What knows a caterpillar
of the butterfly life? The
transformation from the hunger
of Earth to the freedom of air?
What knows the human
of emergence?

And what of the sperm and egg?
From whence do they receive such
nuclear power? What allows them
to begin a new human being?
There is such wild elegance
in cells multiplying by dividing.

We are born in the small
only to grow into the large,
our destiny to return to the tiny.
To that end, transcendent, we
must collect fuel of atomic potency:
those unseen qualities and forces
that spark and sustain our becoming.

Longing

Letters long to be words and
    words to merge into sentences.
Ideas long to become solid,
    possibilities to become endless.
Numbers long to be combined
    and colors to be differentiated.

Pencils long to be shortened
    and hope to become poems;
like a blank sheet of paper,
    a tree longs to be fulfilled;
after a fulfilling life, the caterpillar
    longs to climb the sky.

Lines long to become spirals,
    comets to be captured;
moons long to become planets,
    planets to become suns;
and every one of us, we,
    we long to become stars.

Into the Woods

When

did you lose   did you gain

the awe   the wonder   the passion

of seeing   of experiencing   of feeling   of sensing

the beauty the ugliness [   ] the verge the essence

of earth   of air   of fire   of water

signs   cadences   tokens

colorfully   powerfully

spiraling?

Prepositional

In the search for truth, start within
    then develop without.
In learning, choose standing under
    rather than standing over.
In teaching, focus on alongside
    rather than ahead.
(For liberty, choose yes;
    for maturity, choose no).

Remember: roots grow down
    and blooms spring up.
For the soul, focus on near;
    for the spirit, on far.
We do not end underneath;
    we are destined to rise above.
(For the sake of posterity:
    choose passion over fashion).

New Year's Message

It's not being alone
that should frighten us—
For we are never truly isolated:
aren't the oaks and birches
   and pines our friends?
Don't the stones want to
   come out and play?
Aren't the sounds and breezes
   hoping to catch our ears?

It's not being alone
that should frighten us—
Some of our best friends are
   books and movies and stories,
some of our favorite memories
   don't have to be our own.
No matter, we can befriend ideas.

It's not being alone
that should frighten us—
   Family is always nearby:
Father Sun, Mother Earth, Big Sister Moon,
all the celestial bodies of the firmament,
   and all our younger siblings:
brother crow, sister butterfly,
   brother fox, sister robin.

`

It's not being alone
that should frighten us—
Even our cousins abound:
    milkweed and dandelion,
mullein and daffodil,
    magnolia and dahlia.

It's not being alone
that should frighten us—
It's feeling lost in a new year
    when we are surrounded
by friends and family
    and recognize it not.

Here's the word for the year: SMILE.
Smile up at the sun and moon,
Smile at the sycamores and maples,
    the rhododendrons and daises,
the loons and ospreys.
    To our siblings of the sky: smile.
    To our siblings underground: smile.
    To our cousins of the earth: smile.

Smile, know they are there,
know you are not alone
    and never shall be.
Smile to them all, knowing
they already smile back.

The Quest in Questions

*"To live for a moment without a question
is to cease to exist."*
                    ~Stalking Wolf

The human is an instrument
played by the landscape.

No place or destination or
question is excluded from
everything else around it.
There are always questions
behind the questions.

A question starting with "I"
is doomed to failure, for
there is always a "we."

Eliminate edges, diffuse
into the surroundings,
ask questions with passion
and purpose beyond self.

A question is comprehensive
only when seven levels
have been accessed:

Earth
Water
Air
Fire
Soul
Spirit

What about the questions
behind what is *not* asked?
Who will walk the void
in the now for those?

The earth is a reflection of what
needs to be taught; eliminate
edges, diffuse into the temple,
for all we are is presence.

The biggest problem we have
is not asking the eternal question:

What happened here?

Seeker of Connection

"Words, like nature, half reveal
and half conceal the soul within."
~Alfred Lord Tennyson

We find ourselves truly alive,
these moments sacred fires
that awaken within us essences.

We dance in the joy of togetherness
under the canopy of deep wonder,
melding with nature's harmony.

I lose myself in my own projection;
striding barefoot, I step into the
wildness of the onsetting future.

I have danced with shadows for
too long, bound by expectations
and painful permutations.

I shed my cloak of inhibitions,
start listening to the untamed
rhythms in my buoyancy.

With each step, I reclaim my voice
   With each step, I reclaim my power
      With each step, I reclaim my serenity.

In the wild, I find sanctuary
In the wild, I find connection
In the wild, I find home.

I enjoy singing now, unafraid
of discord
I enjoy dancing now, unafraid
of shadows
I sing and dance wild words whenever
I find them on the trail.

Contemplations on a Trail

The path of ancestry
faces the past, but
must help us move forward in truth.
Everything serves
a purpose—even you
especially you—
as a steward on a
developing planet.

Here, in this great
temple of mysteries,
even the tiniest of
creatures are treasured.
They come to us
because we call;
they stay because
we provide witness.

To make peace
with Mother Nature
we must harmonize
with the unseen,
gain strength
from the diversity,
marvel at every
frost-edged needle,
every rimed hoofprint.

Each track and trace
becomes fertile soil;
there are no tombstones
in the Great Church.

A crow watches me
from a high branch,
a connection is created
and we become brothers
for a tiny moment;
in that sacred space
there is no difference
of purpose.

I step to the edge
of the verdance,
feel the movement.
I place my hand
on a tree, announce
myself and my intention
to give service.
My footsteps are light,
my tracks vibrant.
Flowers shall bloom
here after I pass.

Awakening on Top of Mount Lookout

There is a song I hear
upon wakening
not of notes and chords,
melodies and themes,
but of silence.

The orchestral silences
of the mind,
the body,
the spirit and soul.

They are layered
in the stillness,
tangible and vast,
an intricate weave
of fine filaments
there, then not there

Appearing and disappearing
with the soft, slow breaths
of the universe.

And here am I awakened
in the dawn so fortunate
to have touched ever so
briefly the fugitive
twilight of stillness.

The University of Life

There is a saying: As Above, So Below.
It's a mirror that many sages know
And wise people have come to love.
There is a saying: As Below, So Above.

To study the universe, study man;
Trace back to where everything began.
Engineer what happened in reverse:
To study man, study the universe.

Seven Shields

In the beginning of your journey
get yourself steeled.
Assaulted on all sides:
seven arrows, one shield.

Gather light unto yourself
until the darkness narrows.
Radiate into the world:
one shield, seven arrows.

Breathe the gathering glow,
lift a prayer to the night.
Kneel to the Creator,
yellow, red, black, white.

The past and future conjoin,
the sacred and silent are wed.
The ceremony spins,
black, white, yellow, red.

From northern mountains
to southern meadows,
empty your differences,
reds, blacks, whites, yellows.

The difference between
spirit and flesh contracts.
We are all one people,
whites, yellows, reds, blacks.

When you're dedicated, you'll see
what the unseen yields.
The Way ahead is clear:
one arrow, seven shields.

At the top of the mountain
the road will narrow.
Immortality awaits:
seven shields, one arrow.

Starbound

Where am I going when I pass away?
  Milkweed, mint, juniper, and pine
Remember me as one full of wonder
  Earth was once a love of mine.

Tell Her I enjoyed the walks in the woods
  (with soft loam underneath)
Milkweed, mint, juniper, and pine
  (walking trails few had trodden)
Dappled light through canopy branches,
songbirds encircled my contemplations.

Tell Her I enjoyed the mountain vistas
  (fading blue in maternal majesty)
Milkweed, mint, juniper, and pine
  (the long view and longing already starting)
Deep breaths of fresh, clean air,
open skies full of simple serenity.

Tell Her I enjoyed the fields of emerald green
  (rustling through the tall grass)
Milkweed, mint, juniper, and pine
  (imminent discovery always abounding)
The chorus of life singing out loud
I harmonized as long as I could.

Where am I going when I pass away?
Milkweed, mint, juniper, and pine
Remember me as one full of wonder
Earth was once a love of mine.

Notes on Select Poems

Part I: Moss

"Prelude to the Softer Side"
'Softer' and 'Forest' are interesting anagrams.

"Uplift Walk"
A poem dedicated to my mother, Judy Fischer, which I read at her funeral.

"Stars"
'Star' and 'Arts' are anagrams. Curious indeed.

"In Quintessence"
Numbers are fascinating, each with its own personality.
"One, it has begun."
"Two is the glue."
"Three is the key."
"Four is the door."
"Five comes alive."

"We Can Be Marvelous Together"
I love the idea of "compound interest" as it applies to awareness and being interested in the world around us. The more interest we show in something, the more interesting it becomes.

"A Step in the Right Direction"
There are many teachings about the four directions.

FOUR, though, is cyclical in nature, so it appears in many guises.

"The Oak Speaks"
This is how I think trees would communicate—in words, anyway—ringed and repetitive, with declarations.

"Winter Speaks"
Everything speaks if we could but listen.

Part II: Mind

"Prayer to Childhood"
Inspired by the Prayer of St. Francis.

"Concentric Circles"
Everything ripples. Everything.

"My Listening Stone"
Everyone could use a listening stone.

"Vowels"
'Vowels' and 'Wolves' are anagrams.

"anyone went to a silver why school"
Inspired by "anyone lived in a pretty how town" by E. E. Cummings.

"The Alchemy of Numbers"
There's a lot not said here, a lot to be researched.

"Poem of Gratitude for Some of My Favorite Teachers"
This makes for a great assignment for young poets, to write their own version.

"Star Wise"
Inspired by the Tao Te Ching.

Part III: Mystery

"Reveilations"
Inspired by *Clothed with the Sun* by Anna Kingsford.

"The Old Listeners"
"Sereene" is an invented word. In my mind, a mix of serene and Essenes, the name of the mystical sect from Qumran.

"Fire-By-Friction"
Trees are literally pillars of sunlight. Let that sink in and solidify.

"Transcendence"
Inspired by one of my favorite books, *The Seven Mysteries of Life* by Guy Murchie.

"Into the Woods"
Inspired by "Obligations 2" by Layli Long Soldier.

"New Year's Message"
Or a message for any day.

"The Quest in Questions"
Based on classes I took at Tracker School.

"Seven Shields"
'Shield' anagrams to 'is held' and can be thought of as a principle or standard. And a standard can be thought of as a 'stand hard.'

"Starbound"
Inspired by the traditional ballad "Scarborough Fair." These are four plants that are important to me.

Acknowledgments

Many special thank-yous to my writing companions over the years who pushed me to do weekly assignments and spontaneous on-demand writings and for encouraging my study of words and language at much deeper levels. You know who you are. Thanks to all my students who help keep me excited about teaching and learning. Thank you to Alison Gulotta for editing and making amazing suggestions, and to Eliza Foster for final edits.

Thank you to Nick Zelinger, Judith Briles, and Author U for helping to bring my projects to life.

Also by
Charles Ames Fischer

Creative Thinking Cards

Creative Thinking Cards is the first deck in a series and contains 50 cards for all manner of creative enterprises. As the flagship set, they come with a 42-page explanatory booklet full of useful prompts and ideas. These cards will change the way you see everything!

- Learn new strategies for creative thinking.
- Explore hundreds of ideas and combinations.
- Prompt creativity in powerful, collaborative ways.

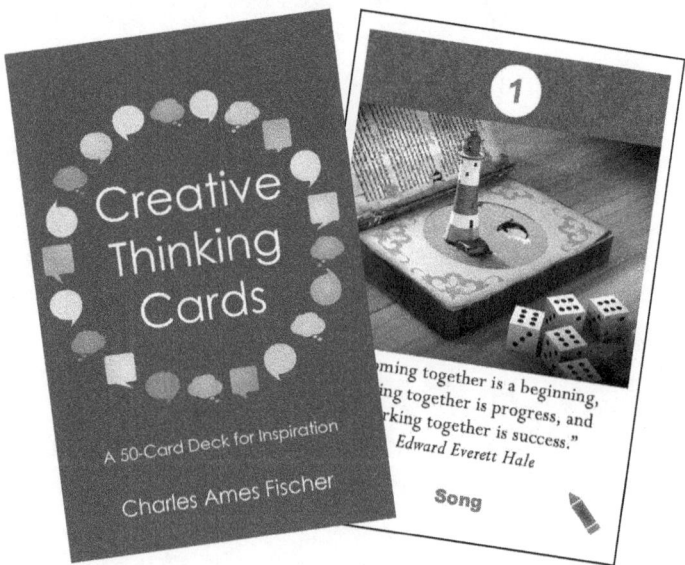

Beyond Infinity

What if numbers came alive? When Matthew discovers a weird computer and a secret door at school, a series of events unfolds where he and his friends solve one mathematical puzzle after another to save 57 and other numbers. *Beyond Infinity* is a fun mathematical MG/YA adventure novel.

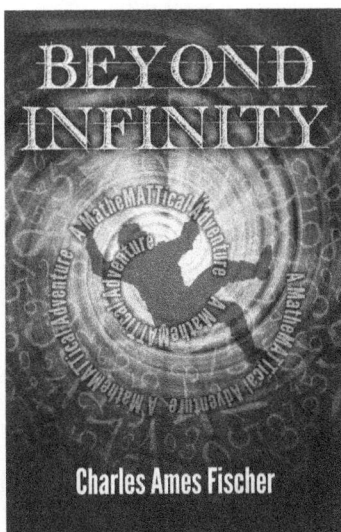

Light the Lamp

Light the Lamp is a collection of forty poems inspired by sports ranging from archery to wrestling. Do some flip turns through these pages and discover how each poem hits the links between the wonderful world of sports and the whimsical words of poetry. Step up to the plate, get the ball rolling, and light the lamp of your imagination. Be a good sport and pick up this book!

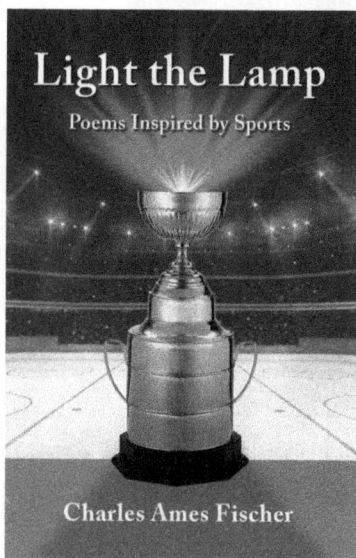

The Power of the Socratic Classroom

In a Socratic Classroom, teachers shift to the role of facilitator, where they help their students develop the collaborative interpersonal skills, the critical and creative thinking skills, and the speaking and listening skills to face the upcoming challenges of the 21st century. This is the definitive guide to facilitating dialogue in any classroom.

About the Author

Charles Ames Fischer has been a teacher for over 25 years. He's called an audible on a few occasions, stepping out of the classroom to be an education consultant. His flagship book, *The Power of the Socratic Classroom,* won four awards and is hands down one of the most complete guidebooks for facilitating dialogue in K to 12 classrooms. He has also written a novel, *Beyond Infinity,* and created a trio of card decks: *Creative Thinking Cards, Creative Thinking Cards: Zany Edition*, and *Nauticara Story-World Cards.* This is his second collection of poems, after *Light the Lamp: Poems Inspired by Sports.*

He enjoys spending time outdoors, reading middle grades books, watching hockey games and contemplating the meaning of life. Fantasy books? They're his secret wilderness.

Working With Me

As a consultant and writing coach, Charles offers numerous writing and thinking classes, professional development workshops, Zoom meetings, and more. His primary expertise is Socratic Seminar, with many related areas, such as critical & creative thinking, active listening, close reading, and asking better questions. Under his guidance, teachers can create spaces where curiosity grows and students discover more than they ever imagined.

As an author, Charles is available for school visits, connecting on Zoom, and for book signings. His specialty is helping others discover the deep roots of writing and the wide branches of reading, and helping students reach further than they ever thought possible Learn more at: *CharlesAmesFischer.com.*